Meet me on™

TIMELESS IMAGES AND FLAVORFUL RECIPES
FROM FLORIDA'S REMARKABLE SCENIC HIGHWAY 30A

*Thanks for
sharing your
Paradise*

*Terry
2018*

Copyright © 2014 by
Southwestern Publishing Group, Inc.

Published by

An imprint of

P.O. Box 305142
Nashville, Tennessee 37230
1-800-358-0560
www.historichospitalitybooks.com

Publisher and President: Dave Kempf
Editorial Director: Mary Cummings
Art Director and Book Design:
Starletta Polster

Library of Congress Control Number: 2014936625
ISBN: 978-0-87197-628-4

Printed in the United States of America

30A.com owner: Mike Ragsdale
Editor and writer: Susan Vallée

Photography: © 30A.com — all pages except where indicated.

Photography by Lauren Alsobrook, pages 58, 70-71

Photography by Brandon Babineaux Photography, cover and
pages 3, 6-7, 16-17, 20, 26, 27, 28 (right), 29, 31 (top right,
bottom right), 37, 40, 41, 42, 43, 46, 47, 48-49, 50-51, 52, 60
(top left), 61, 69, 76 (middle), 78, 82-83, 84-85

Photography by Jamie Conley, pages 18-19, 21, 22-23, 25, 86-87

Photography by Tommy Crow Photography, page 30, 31 (left)

Photography by Jack Gardner, page 36

Photography by Goode Green: Sheila Goode, pages 66 (top
right), 106-107, 114-119, 120

Photography by Ocean Jewels Images, pages 4, 11, 14-15, 56, 57,
59, 60 (bottom), 66-67 (background), 74, 76 (bottom right), 77,
92, 106, 124-125

Photography by Paul Johnson Photography pages 44, 93, 122-123

Photography by Sandestin, pages 98, 100, 101, 102, 103

Photography by Seaside, pages 60 (top right), 66 (top left)

Photography by Jay Thomas, page 63

Photography by Jacqueline Ward, pages 68, 94, 95

Photography by Dawn ChapmanWhitty, page 88

Photography © iStockphoto.com page 89

Sea Oats background photography © Thinkstock

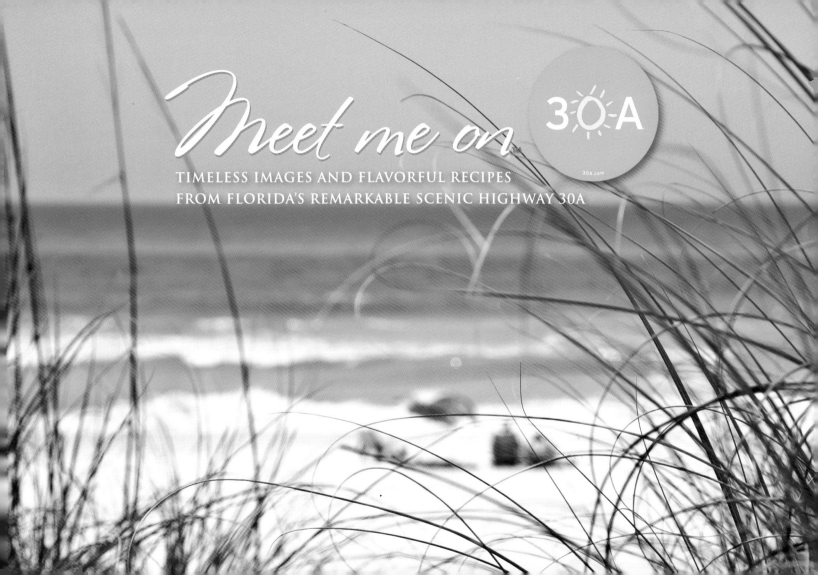

Meet me on

30A

TIMELESS IMAGES AND FLAVORFUL RECIPES
FROM FLORIDA'S REMARKABLE SCENIC HIGHWAY 30A

INTRODUCTION

Dear Reader,

In creating our *Historic Hospitality*® series of books, it is my sincere desire, as publisher, to present beautifully crafted books that relate the cherished history of each geographic area, highlight beautiful historic and contemporary photography, and offer delicious recipes unique to the area. These make the perfect memoir of your visit or a very special gift for a friend. We are proud to include the 30A lifestyle beach communities as one of our featured Historic Hospitality sites.

It is our pleasure to share the story of Scenic 30A with you.

Sincerely,

David J. Kempf

Dave Kempf
Southwestern Publishing Group, Inc.

"A REMARKABLE LABORATORY OF LIFESTYLE."
— *Travel + Leisure* magazine

Welcome to Paradise
Welcome to 30A

Since the beginning of time, mankind has demonstrated a special knack for ruining a perfectly decent Paradise. It seems to be somehow ingrained into our genetic code. As picture-perfect as any place may be, we believe that we can somehow improve upon it.

That's always been the problem with writing about an "undiscovered" piece of pristine paradise—as soon as folks learn about it, you can bet that it won't be too long before there are condo towers, water slides, goofy golfs and cannons blasting off to spoil an otherwise serene sunset. Time and time again, Paradise is lost to greed or a general lack of vision.

But it would be tough to argue that Florida's Scenic Highway 30A hasn't already been discovered. Even though our community only has 12,000 full-time residents, some 3 million people visit this area every year.

Although 30A itself may no longer be a secret, there's certainly a secret formula behind its success. 30A hasn't somehow magically "retained" its charm. Its charm has been crafted; cultivated. It didn't happen by accident. In fact, it's all by design.

In too many vacation destinations, Mother Nature is forced to take a backseat to neon-touted man-made attractions. Instead, locals here enthusiastically embrace the simple splendor of the great outdoors. Rather than paving paradise, visionaries sought early on to protect it. In fact, 40 percent of the land on this peninsula between the Gulf of Mexico and Choctawhatchee Bay is protected habitat. That means there's over 25,000 acres of undeveloped land to explore by foot, bike or waterway.

Rather than high-rises, Seaside's brilliant "small town" design was crafted with quaint neighborly cottages, beach pavilions, cobblestone streets, white picket fences, and picture-perfect parks. Nearby 30A neighborhoods adopted these same "New Urbanist" principles.

People might think they're coming here for the beach, but if that was the primary driving factor, they can certainly find better Gulf views from condo high-rises in other places. Instead, people come here to immerse themselves in nature and 30A's nostalgic sense of community. They come for picnics in the park, bike rides along cobblestone streets and concerts under the stars.

With pristine natural beauty as our setting, extraordinary architecture and urban design as the stage, and an eclectic bevy of talents as our locals, 30A is enjoying a coastal renaissance—an explosion of musical, artistic, entrepreneurial and culinary creativity.

Travel + Leisure magazine once called 30A "one of the most intriguing stretches of roadway in America" and a "remarkable laboratory of lifestyle."

We agree… and it's all by design.

Mike Ragsdale — 30A.com

Contents

SCENIC HIGHWAY 30A

Scenic Highway 30A is a remarkable driving experience. The little two-lane road winds through beach towns, giving glimpses of the emerald green waters of the Gulf of Mexico and offering astounding views of rare coastal dune lakes.

But what exactly is 30A? Is it just a pretty drive? An architectural curiosity? We think not. Locals will tell you that this is where they came to find themselves. This is where businesses were launched, creative dreams were fulfilled and life finally slowed down for them. The 30A life is a place where toasting sunset, cheering on friends in a paddle board contest or seeing familiar faces every where you go is routine. It is also the sheer beauty of this place. Rare coastal dune lakes defy imagination when their sweet tea-colored waters break through the dunes, spilling out into the welcoming blue waves with a force so sudden it will knock you off your feet. It's the acres upon acres of state forest, the delight of fine cuisine on a balmy August evening and bonding with strangers as a bell tolls at the end of the day. 30A is not simply a place.

It is a lifestyle, a spirit and a way of being.

◄ DESTIN   PANAMA CITY ►

FLORIDA

Baytowne Wharf

Grand Blvd

Santa Rosa Beach

331

Pt. Washington

Miramar Beach

Sandestin

TOPS'L

30A

393

83

283

395

98

NatureWalk

Dune Allen

Gulf Place

Blue Mountain Beach

Grayton Beach

WaterColor

Seaside

Seagrove

30A

WaterSound

Alys Beach

Seacrest

Rosemary Beach

Inlet Beach

30A

GULF OF MEXICO

A guide to hiking and biking in South Walton

Do you feel like venturing out for a relaxing hike or bike ride? Within South Walton are 200 miles of hiking and biking trails that wind through state forest, state parks, and Scenic 30A. Gob-smacking views of coastal dune lakes, the Gulf of Mexico, scrub oak, endangered birds and local architecture are the reward for swapping flip flops for hiking shoes.

TIMPOOCHEE TRAIL

Want to really sound like an old-timer? Refer to the 30A bike path using its real name—the Timpoochee Trail. Named for Timpoochee Kinnard (an influential Indian Chief of the Euchee Indian tribe), this paved path meanders its way along the entire length of Scenic Highway 30A. Hop on a bike, grab some water and get ready to explore the 19 miles of the trail. You'll cross coastal dune lakes, state parks and beautiful 30A communities.

TOPSAIL HILL PRESERVE STATE PARK

At the far end of Scenic Highway 30A are 1,600 acres of protected bald cypress swamps, sand dunes, beachfront and two freshwater coastal dune lakes. The serene beachfront and top-notch state park facilities make Topsail Hill a great place to spend the entire day. Seven trails vary from easy to difficult. Be sure to ask the park rangers about the five rare plant species that are only found within Topsail Hill — and then see if you can spot them.

A fee is required to enter the park and a tram will take you right to the beach.

POINT WASHINGTON STATE FOREST TRAILS

If you feel like getting off the beaten path and experiencing the "real" Florida forest, pick a trail within the Point Washington State Forest system. There are more than 27 miles of trails that transverse the 15,000-acre state forest. Trails vary from easy to difficult and will lead you through longleaf pine flat woods, sandhills, coastal scrub and wetland areas. Along the way you might spot wild boar, deer, gopher tortoise or the white-topped pitcher plant.

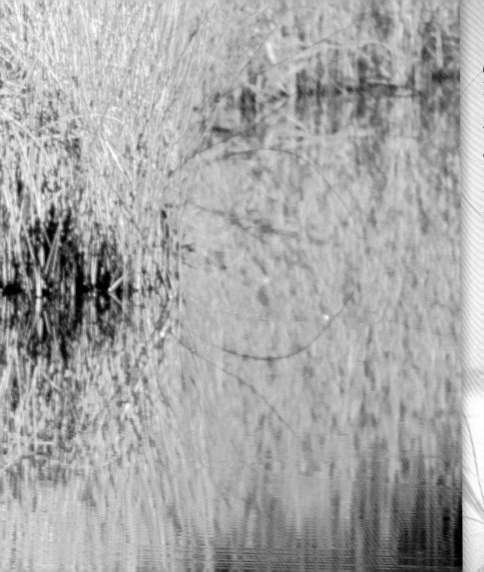

GRAYTON BEACH STATE RECREATION AREA

If you are staying in Seaside or WaterColor, then you are probably aware of Grayton Beach State Park (because it is located on the other side of Western Lake). What you might not realize, however, is how removed you can feel from the hustle and bustle of 30A while exploring the trails along the lake's shore or from a stand-up paddle board. For a nominal fee, you can enjoy the solitude of the park's beaches and two easy-to-moderate hiking trails. And be sure to look for the prayer of the woods that is hidden beneath a dune canopy.

KELLOGG NATURE CENTER

On the north side of County Highway 393 (north of Gulf Place) is a 10-acre parcel of land that will soon be converted to a nature preserve and nature center. A short trail is marked and is a nice spot for bird watching.

30A *Tip*

ENJOY ACRES OF
UNSPOILED DUNE HABITAT
AT THE INLET BEACH
PUBLIC GULF-FRONT PARK.
IT'S ALSO A GREAT
SPOT FOR BEACH
WEDDINGS.

INLET BEACH

Inlet Beach is the "blink-and-you-missed-it" entrance to Scenic 30A on the eastern end of South Walton. This sleepy little community experienced a boom in growth after World War II when the Bureau of Land Development gave soldiers returning from the war the opportunity to enter a lottery for beachfront property. While Inlet Beach is chopped in half by US Highway 98, the outstanding beauty of Lake Powell, Camp Helen State Park and South Walton's largest Gulf-front park is undeniable.

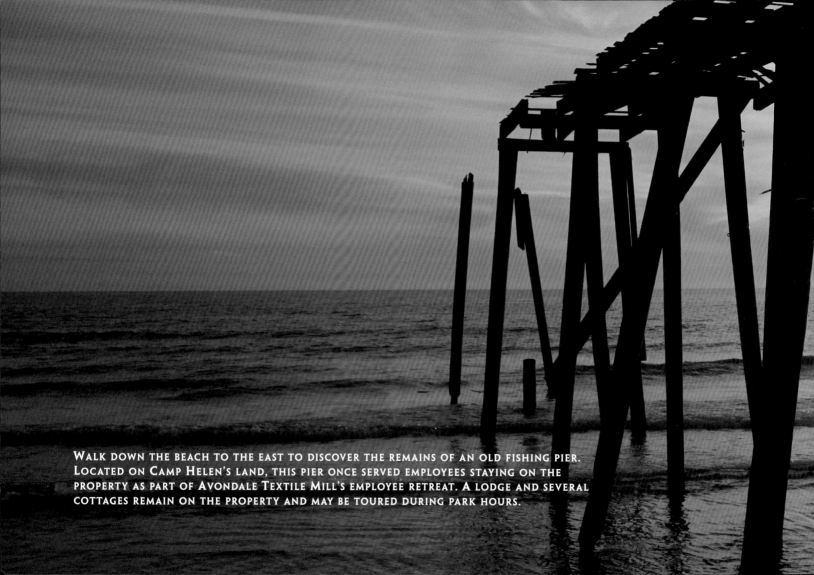

WALK DOWN THE BEACH TO THE EAST TO DISCOVER THE REMAINS OF AN OLD FISHING PIER. LOCATED ON CAMP HELEN'S LAND, THIS PIER ONCE SERVED EMPLOYEES STAYING ON THE PROPERTY AS PART OF AVONDALE TEXTILE MILL'S EMPLOYEE RETREAT. A LODGE AND SEVERAL COTTAGES REMAIN ON THE PROPERTY AND MAY BE TOURED DURING PARK HOURS.

Baked Crab Dip

Shades Restaurant — Chef Greg Wakeham
Inlet Beach

3 (8-ounce) packages cream cheese, softened
1/4 cup minced garlic
1/4 cup lemon juice
1 1/2 tablespoon blackened seasoning
1 1/2 tablespoons Old Bay seasoning
1 tablespoon Worcestershire sauce
10 cups mayonnaise
2 cans lump crab meat
2 cans claw crab meat
Grated cheese

Combine the cream cheese and seasonings in a large bowl; mix well. Add the mayonnaise. Beat at low speed of an electric mixer until blended. Fold in the seafood. Spoon into a large ovenproof serving dish. Sprinkle with grated cheese. Bake at 325 degrees until heated through.

Serves a crowd

ROSEMARY BEACH

*V*isitors to Rosemary Beach often comment on the unexpected old world charm of this beach front town. Cobblestone streets, old-fashioned gas lamps, oak-lined streets and architecture inspired by the historic homes of St. Augustine and the Caribbean combine to create one of 30A's most beautiful beach communities.

It is a town whose population swells during the summer, but still feels quiet and secluded. A downtown shopping area surrounds a park on both sides of 30A. Here you will find the Town Hall (a popular spot for weddings) and a collection of fine dining, boutique clothing shops, toy stores, a book store, a coffee shop, day spa, a bank and a luxurious 55-room hotel.

Dining options include freshly caught fish (of course!), Gulf shrimp, Spanish tapas, Italian cuisine, hand-cut steaks, homemade dips and spreads, organic coffees and an entire shop filled with candy. Everything you need to go about your day is here, which is why so many Rosemary Beach vacationers turn into Rosemary Beach homeowners.

The 107-acre town was master planned by DPZ, the same design team that planned neighboring Alys Beach and Seaside. There are numerous parks and greens where children can play and events are held. A thriving tennis center is located just across the street from a gym and covered swimming pool, and a wooden boardwalk system leads to dune walkovers and the unforgettable white sand beaches. Most of the homes in Rosemary Beach are designed with private courtyards. These provide restful spaces for the family to gather for a swim or an outdoor barbecue after a long day spent at the beach, and most are landscaped with blooming flowers, climbing vines and bubbling fountains.

Once the sun sets in Rosemary Beach, the town is transformed. Flickering gas lamps and an arcade of trees light up — creating a magical place to run in the grass. You'll see people carrying glasses of wine and picnic baskets down Main Street to formally toast sunset. In fact, sunset toasts are so popular, the town's beach chair provider had to create a special sunset beach service (two chairs and a small table) for a comfortable spot to watch the show.

The town's homeowners are thoroughly invested in Rosemary. It was a small group of homeowners who created the Ohana Institute, a private school for students in 5th through 12th grade. And a non-profit organization called Rosemary Beach Foundation sponsors cultural events throughout the year.

Ongoing yearly activities include outdoor ballet performances, movies, wine festivals, kids' "rock the block" parties, outdoor theatre, a farmers market and live outdoor concerts. It's the type of town where luxury waits at every turn and nothing is rushed or overlooked.

The Pearl — Rosemary Beach

HAVANA BEACH BAR AND GRILL AT THE PEARL

Cuban Tostones with Havana Mojo Sauce

Havana Beach Bar and Grill at the Pearl — EXECUTIVE CHEF MICHAEL GUERRA

ROSEMARY BEACH

FOR THE TOSTONES

Plantains, peeled   *Salt to taste*
Oil for deep frying

Cut the plantains into 2-inch sections. Deep-fry until golden brown; drain. Chill in the refrigerator. Smash plantains with hands to flatten. Deep-fry until crispy; drain. Season with salt. Serve with Havana Mojo Sauce.

HAVANA MOJO SAUCE

1	*cup olive oil*		1	*tablespoon grated orange zest*
1/4	*cup fresh lime juice*		1	*tablespoon fresh oregano*
1	*cup orange juice*		2	*teaspoons ground cumin*
1/4	*cup chopped cilantro*		1 1/2	*teaspoons salt*
2	*ounces minced garlic*		1 1/2	*teaspoons ground black pepper*

Combine all ingredients in a medium bowl. Whisk until well mixed. Serve with the tostones.

Makes about 2 1/2 cups

Cajun Remoulade Sauce

Havana Beach Bar and Grill at the Pearl — EXECUTIVE CHEF MICHAEL GUERRA

ROSEMARY BEACH

3	large red bell peppers		2	cloves of garlic
1	tablespoon plus 2 teaspoons smoked paprika		1/2	teaspoon cayenne pepper
3	tablespoons red wine vinegar		2	cups mayonnaise
1	tablespoon Dijon mustard			

Roast the red peppers on the grill or in the oven until charred black. Place in a bowl; cover with plastic wrap. Let stand until the peppers have cooled.

Peel off the charred skin and remove the seed. Place in a blender with the paprika, red wine vinegar, mustard, garlic, and cayenne pepper. Purée until smooth. Combine with the mayonnaise in a bowl; mix well. Store in the refrigerator. Serve with fried seafood.

Makes about 3 cups

"French French" Toast

Summer Kitchen Cafe
ROSEMARY BEACH

1 24-inch French baguette	2 large eggs, beaten
Juice and grated zest of 1 orange	1 teaspoon pure vanilla extract
1 cup milk, almond milk or coconut milk	Coconut oil, olive oil or butter for searing
(have fun with dairy-like ingredients)	Confectioner's sugar, strawberries and maple syrup
2 tablespoons sugar	for garnishing

Cut the baguette on the bias into 2-inch thick slices. Combine the orange juice, zest, milk and sugar in a dish, stirring to dissolve the sugar. Add the eggs and vanilla; mix well. Preheat a sheet pan in a 350-degree oven. Dip the bread slices on both sides one at a time into the egg mixture. Squeeze out excess with tongs; do not over squeeze. Sauté in butter in a skillet until brown; turn. Sauté until light brown. Place light brown side up on the preheated sheet pan. Repeat with the remaining bread.

Bake until crisp on the outside but still moist in the center. Place on individual plates. Top with the confectioner's sugar, strawberry garnish and maple syrup.

Makes 12 slices

Mushroom Caps

La Crema Tapas & Chocolate
ROSEMARY BEACH

1/2 cup minced shallots	20 finely chopped lobster tails	3 spoonfuls lobster base
Clarified butter	3 pounds of cream cheese	Cremini mushrooms

Sauté the shallots in clarified butter until translucent. Add the lobster meat. Sauté until cooked through. Stir in the lobster base and cream cheese. Cook until the ingredients are mixed well, stirring constantly. Let stand until cool. Scoop out the mushroom gills with the back of a spoon. Fill with lobster filling. Drizzle each with enough clarified butter to cover. Let stand until the butter hardens. Bake on a parchment-lined baking pan at 400 degrees for 8 minutes or until lightly browned.

Serves 4

Churros

1 cup margarine	1/2 teaspoon salt	Cinnamon-sugar to coat
2 cups plus 1 tablespoon flour	6 eggs	Dipping chocolate, prepared

Bring 2 cups water and margarine to a rolling boil in a saucepan. Stir in a mixture of the flour and salt; reduce heat to low. Stir vigorously for about 1 minute or until the mixture forms as ball. Remove from the heat. Beat in the eggs vigorously one at a time. Chill for 2 hours or longer. Pipe small pieces from a pastry bag into hot oil. Deep-fry until browned. Drain and roll in cinnamon-sugar. Dip into the dipping chocolate.

Makes about 4 dozen

SEACREST

*I*n between Alys Beach and Rosemary Beach is a colorful and thriving beach community called Seacrest. Close to everything, and yet somehow quite relaxed, Seacrest is an ideal place to reconnect with friends and family. Bikes and flip-flops are the transportation of choice here, except for the occasional golf cart loaded up with kids, coolers, umbrellas and sand buckets.

The "town center" of Seacrest is arguably The Village of South Walton Beach, featuring several cute shops and restaurants, as well as a convenience store. The tiny shops on the green are a hit with barefoot kids and weary parents seeking a momentary diversion from the wait for dinner.

In addition to the Seacrest's gorgeous beaches, there's also a 12,000 square foot swimming pool hidden in the expansive Seacrest neighborhood. One would think that it's difficult to "hide" a 12,000 square foot pool, and yet, Seacrest somehow pulled it off. If you can find it (and if you're a property homeowner or rental guest), it's certainly worth checking out.

SEACREST BEACH POOL

Chef Ben's Chili Relleno

La Cocina Mexican Bar and Grill
SEACREST BEACH

4	poblano peppers		1	teaspoon salt
1	tablespoon cooking oil		1/2	teaspoon pepper
1/2	cup finely chopped onion		1/2	teaspoon cinnamon
1	pound lean ground beef		1	cup sour cream
1	cup tomato sauce		1/2	cup walnuts
1/2	cup each minced dried apricots, golden raisins, and walnuts		1/2	cup sugar
			1	teaspoon powdered chicken consommé
1/2	cup honey		Pomegranate seeds for garnishing	
1	tablespoon powdered chicken consommé			

Rub the poblano peppers with a small amount of cooking oil. Roast over an open flame, turning until all sides are charred. Place in a tightly covered container. Let stand until cool. Peel, cut a slit in the side and remove the seeds and membranes. Sauté the onion in the remaining oil in a medium skillet on medium high heat until translucent. Add the ground beef. Cook until browned and cooked through, stirring frequently; drain. Add the tomato sauce, dried fruits, walnuts, honey, 1 tablespoon powdered consommé and seasonings. Simmer for 5 minutes on low heat, stirring constantly. Remove from the heat. Fill each pepper with the ground beef mixture, being careful not to split the peppers. Place on a serving plate. Combine the sour cream and remaining ingredients in a blender or food processor. Process until thoroughly combined. Top each pepper with about 1/4 cup of the sauce. Garnish with pomegranate seeds.

Serves 4

Wild Mushroom and Rice Balls

Acme Ice House — CHEF NATE LINCK
SEACREST BEACH

6	tablespoons melted unsalted butter		1/3	cup chopped parsley
1	teaspoon olive oil		2	cups shredded asiago cheese
1/4	cup minced yellow onion		3	tablespoons kosher salt
2	tablespoons minced garlic		1	teaspoon black pepper
4	cups arborio rice		20	(1/2-inch) cubes fontina cheese
1/3	cup white wine		4	cups all-purpose flour
12	cups hot chicken broth		4	cups beaten eggs
2	cups sautéed mushrooms		4	cups Japanese bread crumbs
2	cups sautéed leeks			Oil for deep frying

In a mixture of the butter and olive oil, sauté the minced yellow onion and garlic until translucent. Stir in the rice until coated. Sauté until the edges of the rice become clear. Add the wine. Cook until the wine has almost evaporated. Add the chicken broth to the rice 1 ladleful at a time, stirring and cooking after each addition until the rice is al dente when tasted. Add the mushrooms, leeks, parsley and asiago cheese; mix well. Season with salt and pepper to taste. Cook for 5 minutes longer or until the rice is tender. Spread onto a sheet pan to cool. Scoop the rice mixture into balls with an ice cream scoop, pressing with your palm to eliminate excess. Create an impression in the center of the rice with your thumb. Place 1 cube of the fontina cheese into each ball and pinch to close. Roll the rice back into a ball. Roll each ball in the flour, dip into the eggs, and coat with the bread crumbs. Deep-fry in 300-degree oil for 11 minutes. Serve over tomato sauce and garnish with Parmesan cheese and parsley on top

Makes 6 servings.

ALYS BEACH

Alys Beach is one of 30A's most exciting new towns. This visually stunning place is comprised of all-white buildings accented by colored shutters and lush green courtyards. As you enter Alys Beach, you are greeted by two massive buildings (called the Butteries) which border the 30A bike path. These butteries are inspired by traditional Bermudan structures that housed butter and milk. While these don't store butter or milk, they do contain interesting tile mosaics which reflect local history of the area.

The majority of the homes in Alys Beach are designed with a private interior courtyard and front narrow stone pathways. These rock solid homes are constructed with solid masonry walls and roofs to create the world's first *FORTIFIED for Safer Living*™ community (an insurance industry standard).

This town in the making was designed by DPZ, the same award-winning planners that designed neighboring Rosemary Beach and Seaside. A large amphitheater and distinctive pocket parks accentuate the community and surround Caliza Pool. This Moroccan-inspired oasis takes relaxing poolside to a luxurious level never before seen on 30A. Three pools: a shaded family pool, a 75-foot lap pool (with underwater musical selections) and an infinity edge 100-foot saltwater pool comprise the heart of Caliza. A small bar and restaurant provides refreshments during the day and serves world-class meals at night. Caliza is a sight to be seen.

CALIZA POOL

30A *Tip*

JUST NORTH OF CALIZA
IS ALYS BEACH'S 20-ACRE
NATURE PRESERVE. HERE YOU
CAN ENJOY A WOODED WALK
THROUGH WETLAND AREAS,
ALLOWING FOR BEAUTIFUL
VIEWS OF PITCHER PLANTS
AND CYPRESS TREES
FROM AN ELEVATED
BOARDWALK.

Sesame Crab and Avocado

George's at Alys Beach

ALYS BEACH

FOR EACH SERVING

Jumbo lump crab meat
Diced avocado
1   part sesame oil
1   part tamari or soy sauce
2   parts canola oil
Black and white sesame seeds to taste

Organic spring greens
Chopped red onion
Whole grape tomatoes
Chopped yellow tomato
Chopped cucumber

Combine the crab meat and avocado in a bowl; toss lightly. Add enough of a mixture of the sesame oil, tamari, canola oil, and sesame seeds to coat; mix lightly.

Combine the spring greens, red onion, grape tomatoes, yellow tomato, and cucumber on a serving plate. Spoon the crab meat mixture on top.

WATERSOUND

While the homes, bridges, beach club, pool and trails of the WaterSound community are private and gated, the restaurants and shops at the entrance are not. A family-run pizzeria is a great place to grab a bite to eat while taking a break from biking down 30A's bike path. Located next "door" to WaterSound is Deer Lake State Park. Here you'll find undisturbed beaches and a fantastic series of trails. You can also enjoy views of WaterSound's coastal lake inlet from the bike path.

Camp Creek Lake also borders the community. It is a popular spot to stop for sunset photos, so don't be alarmed if you notice cars suddenly pulling over on the bridge. Sometimes those sunsets are so breathtaking you just have to pull over the car and take a moment to soak it in.

WATERSOUND

DEER LAKE STATE PARK HIKING TRAIL

I bet you never thought you'd be excited to spot a mouse on the beach, did you? At Deer Lake State Park you can look for the Choctawhatchee beach mouse, a small light-colored mouse that is an endangered species. The mouse prefers to nest within the sand dunes and helps the dune system thrive by spreading the seeds of sea oats and other grasses.

THESE OATS AND GRASSES FORTIFY THE DUNES DURING STORMS AND HURRICANES.

DEER LAKE

Seagrove Beach

C.H. McGee doesn't get a lot of credit for shaping the style of 30A, but he should. After World War II, the real estate developer took the 80 acres that he owned and created a community with strict covenants that would keep "trailer, tent, shack, outhouse or other temporary structures" out and single family homes in. Disgusted by the rampant growth he was seeing in nearby Panama City Beach, McGee worked hard to create a self sufficient town. At the heart of this heavily shaded paradise was Seagrove Village Market Café grocery store and gas station. While it no longer sells gas, the Market is one of the most popular restaurants on 30A. Just head towards the back of the store, and place your order like a local. You pay on the way out of the store.

Longhorn Mac 'n' Cheese

Cowgirl Kitchen
SEAGROVE BEACH & ROSEMARY BEACH

1¹/2 cups butter
1¹/2 cups flour
1¹/2 tablespoons salt
4   quarts (16 cups) heavy cream

1   cup grated queso or white American cheese
5   cups grated mild Cheddar cheese
4   pounds elbow macaroni pasta
Shredded sharp Cheddar cheese for topping

Melt the butter in a heavy saucepan over medium heat. Whisk in the flour and salt gradually to make a roux. Add the heavy cream gradually, whisking constantly until all the cream is incorporated. Simmer until of a medium white sauce consistency. Add the queso and mild Cheddar cheeses. Cook until cheese melts, stirring constantly; set aside.

Cook the pasta in a large pot of boiling water using package directions or until just tender. Pour into a colander. Rinse under running water to remove all the starch; drain well. Add to the white sauce; mix well. Spoon into a large greased casserole. Top with a generous amount of shredded sharp Cheddar cheese. Bake at 350 degrees until hot and bubbly and the cheese topping melts.

Serves a crowd

Grilled Fish with Stewed White Beans, Arugula and Tomatoes

723 Whiskey Bravo
SEAGROVE BEACH

8 ounces Applewood smoked bacon, cut into quarters	2 tablespoons salt
1 small yellow onion, diced	1 tablespoon black pepper
3 pounds dried white beans	1 cup diced tomato
1/4 cup high quality chicken base	2 cups fresh arugula
8 cups water	Fresh Grilled Fish

Sauté the bacon in a large stockpot until just beginning to crisp. Add the onion, stirring to scrape the bottom of the stockpot. Cook for 5 minutes longer or until the onions are soft. Add the beans, chicken base, water and seasoning. Bring to a boil; reduce the heat to medium low. Simmer for about 1 hour or until the beans no longer float, stirring and checking for liquid frequently.

Simmer for about 25 to 30 minutes longer or until the beans are soft. Add the tomato and arugula just before serving. Heat for several minutes or until arugula wilts. Serve with your favorite grilled fresh fish.

Serves 4

EDEN GARDENS STATE PARK

You have to venture off of 30A for a visit to Eden State Garden's Wesley House. Built in the 1800s by the Wesley's, a wealthy timber family, it was renovated in 1963 by Lois Maxon who donated her personal collection of Louis XVI furniture to the state. Thanks to her generosity, the Wesley House is home to the second largest collection of Louis XVI furniture in the country.

Tours of the home are given Thursday through Monday from 10 a.m.—3 p.m. for a small fee.

Surrounding the home are 161 acres of unspoiled woods, the shores of the Choctawhatchee Bay, and the carefully manicured lawns and reflecting pool of the estate. The lawn outside of the Wesley House has become such a popular spot for weddings that the massive Live Oak tree on the grounds has been dubbed "the wedding tree."

A series of nature trails cuts through the Old Florida landscape, providing you the opportunity to stop and listen and experience what South Walton was like before it was discovered by the masses. Picnic tables border the Bay along one nature trail, while another crosses over a small bridge.

Behind the Wesley House is the rose garden, another popular location for weddings. Take a close look at the brick pavers and see if you can figure out where they came from.

30A *Tip*
For one of the best photos, stand north of the reflecting pond to capture the home's image in the still waters.

THE LAWN OUTSIDE OF THE WESLEY HOUSE HAS BECOME SUCH A POPULAR SPOT FOR WEDDINGS THAT THE MASSIVE LIVE OAK TREE ON THE GROUNDS HAS BEEN DUBBED "THE WEDDING TREE."

SEASIDE

3 0A owes much of its popularity to the captivating little town known as Seaside. Its official motto is "A Simple, Beautiful Life," and once you've spent time here you'll understand why. In this New Urbanist town (the first of its kind), priority is given to those who wish to explore and discover. Sandy paths twist and turn throughout Seaside, while beach walkovers act as dramatic gateways to the sea, framing the Gulf of Mexico like oversized works of art.

In Seaside, which was more of a character in "The Truman Show" than a backdrop, time slows, allowing you to enjoy the white-sand beaches while unplugging from the static of everyday life.

Even ordinary moments, like grabbing breakfast or unwinding at the end of the day take on new forms here. Breakfast becomes a peaceful walk towards Central Square for a homemade muffin and a stop at the nearest beach walkover to assess the day's waves.

Laughter on a screened porch at sunset replaces television for the week. A hot, summer day with toes dug into the cool sand of Seaside gets even better with the delivery of slow-roasted barbecue and a Technicolor snow cone bought through the window of a vintage Airstream trailer.

A professional town theatre, concerts on the amphitheater green, monthly art walks and a weekly farmers market ensure that everyone is entertained — and you don't need to move the car once.

Seaside manages to take the moments in life that are truly precious, and amplify them.

The delightful little town was conceived and developed by the husband and wife team of Robert and Daryl Davis. The couple were developing a small housing project in Miami called Apogee when they happened to meet architects Andrés Duany and Elizabeth Plater-Zyberk. Intrigued by what the Davis' were doing, the pair quickly formed a friendship and eventually talk turned to what could be done with the 80 acres of beachfront land Robert's grandfather had left him.

The result would be an architectural movement called New Urbanism and a little town dubbed Seaside. *Time* magazine would later declare it one of the most important architectural achievements of our time.

Throughout the design and building phase Robert encouraged architectural integrity by working with renowned theorist Leon Krier and renowned and up-and-coming architects.

The entire community is walkable with a founding principle being that a child could buy a popsicle near the beach and walk home before it melted.

In Seaside's shopping district you'll find a diverse collection of mom and pop shops and locally owned restaurants. If you have the time, stop by Modica Market for one of their famous sweet teas and go for a walk. The best way to experience Seaside is by foot.

30A Tip

TOWN FOUNDERS
ROBERT AND DARYL DAVIS
WERE MARRIED IN THE
GAZEBO ON TUPELO STREET.
"THE RED HOUSE" WAS ONE
OF THE FIRST HOMES
CONSTRUCTED IN THE
NOW BUILT-OUT
COMMUNITY.

Meet The Queen

Raw & Juicy
Organic Juice Bar and Raw Food Cafe
SEASIDE

3	medium carrots ~anti-cancer + anti-oxidants + clarity of (in)sight
2	oranges, peeled ~ immunity boost
1	lemon ~ alkaline + detox
1	finger-length piece ginger ~ increased digestion + detox

1	finger-length piece Turmeric or 1 tablespoons turmeric powder ~ time tested QUEEN of anti-inflammation
1	young Thai coconut and meat (about 8 ounces juice and ¼ cup coconut meat) or
1	cup bottled coconut water ~ super hydration + electrolyte balance

Juice the carrots, oranges, lemon, ginger and fresh turmeric. Blend the coconut water and meat well in a blender, add turmeric if using dry. Once blended, combine all ingredients in a pitcher and stir.

Voila! Meet the Queen of anti-inflammation, hydration, immunity, and detox.

Taste: Sweet, Sour, Bitter, Pungent + Astringent

Grits A Ya Ya

Great Southern Cafe

SEASIDE

FOR THE GRITS

4	cups chicken stock
2	cups grits such as Dixie Lily
1	cup heavy cream

4	ounces unsalted butter
1	14 to 16-ounce can creamed corn

Shredded smoked Gouda cheese

Bring the chicken stock to a boil in a heavy bottomed saucepan. Sir in the grits. Reduce the heat to low. Simmer for 40 minutes, stirring occasionally. Add the cream, butter, and creamed corn; mix well. Add the cheese. Stir until the cheese melts.

FOR THE SHRIMP YA YA

8	strips Applewood smoked bacon, diced
1	tablespoon each minced garlic and shallots
3	tablespoons unsalted butter

White wine

1	pound peeled and deveined jumbo shrimp

2	cups chopped fresh spinach
1/4	cup diced scallions
1	Portobello mushroom cap, sliced
2	cups heavy cream

Salt and freshly ground black pepper to taste

Hot sauce to taste

Sauté the bacon in a large heated saucepan over medium heat for about 3 minutes. Add the garlic and shallots. Sauté until tender. Add the butter and white wine. Cook until the butter is half melted. Add the shrimp. Cook until the bottom half of the shrimp turn white; turn. Add the spinach, scallions and mushrooms. Sauté for 2 minutes. Remove the shrimp; set aside. Add the heavy cream. Simmer until reduced by 1/3. Season with salt, pepper and hot sauce. Return the shrimp; mix gently. Mound the cheese grits on a plate. Spoon the shrimp mixture over the top.

Seaside Shrimp

Bud and Alley's Waterfront Restaurant and Rooftop Bar
SEASIDE

FOR EACH SERVING

8	head-on shrimp, bodies peeled with head and tail intact
2	teaspoons chopped fresh rosemary
1	teaspoon fresh thyme
1/2	teaspoon coarsely ground black pepper
1	tablespoon chopped garlic
1	tablespoon chopped shallot
1/4	cup blended oil
1/4	cup white wine
1	tablespoon fresh lemon juice
2	roasted tomatoes, crushed
1/2	cup shrimp stock
4	tablespoons (2 ounces) cold butter

Combine the shrimp, rosemary, thyme, pepper, garlic, shallot and oil in a bowl; stir to coat. Marinate for 2 hours. Sauté the shrimp in a medium skillet over medium-high heat just until the shrimp start to turn pink. Add the wine and stir to deglaze the skillet. Add the lemon juice, tomatoes, and shrimp stock.

Cook until liquid is reduced by half. Add the butter and swirl the skillet until the butter is incorporated and the mixture is saucy. Adjust the seasonings and serve in a large bowl with a slice of grilled Tuscan bread.

Just Married
Seaside, FL

WATERCOLOR

aterColor is a beach town with refined tastes and a passion for the outdoors. Lush landscaping and elaborate pocket parks blend seamlessly with Northwest Florida's natural scrub oak and palmetto. WaterColor borders the Gulf of Mexico and Western Lake, South Walton's largest coastal dune lake. When designing the community, care was taken to preserve the health and natural beauty of Western Lake. Instead of immediately bordering the lake, lake-front homes in WaterColor view this rare natural wonder through the shadow of tall pine and scrub oak. Gravel nature trails twist and wind through these woods providing a way for neighbors to connect for a morning walk or bike ride. Elaborate foot bridges criss-cross Western Lake and lead to simple docks and peaceful structures that are the perfect spot for a midday picnic or a moment of quiet reflection. A large butterfly garden on the north side of Scenic 30A leads to an outdoor amphitheater and boathouse. It is at the boathouse that you can discover the sensation of walking on water by trying out a stand up paddle-board or rent a canoe or kayak and paddle toward the shores of Grayton Beach State Park.

On the south side of Scenic 30A is the WaterColor Beach Club and the luxurious WaterColor Inn, home of the James Beard award-winning restaurant, Fish Out of Water. WaterColor Inn has been declared one of the World's Best Hotels by *Travel + Leisure* magazine. Balcony views from the Inn overlook towering sand dunes and miles of pristine white sand in Grayton Beach State Park.

Be sure to walk down the 30A bike path and cross Western Lake. The views from your car window as you drive by are spectacular, but the perception of the water and the views of the Gulf beyond are staggering when seen on foot. And the tall Longleaf Pines that border the south side of Western Lake are one of 30A's most treasured sights.

30A *Tip*

EXPLORE THE BEAUTY OF
CERULEAN PARK. LOCATED JUST
NORTH OF THE WATERCOLOR
CLOCK TOWER, THIS GORGEOUS
GREEN PARK SHOWS OFF THE
TWISTED TRUNKS OF SCRUB OAK
AND AN ARRAY OF NATIVE PLANTS.
A COLORFUL BUTTERFLY GARDEN
IS PLANTED ALONGSIDE A
CASCADING FOUNTAIN THAT
RUNS THE LENGTH OF
THE PARK.

Gulf Black Grouper with Sweet Corn Pudding, Succotash and Blistered Cherry Tomatoes

Fish Out of Water — EXECUTIVE CHEF BRIAN MURRAY

WATERCOLOR

CORN PUDDING

1 cup vegetable stock
Kernels from 3 ears of corn
Kosher salt and black pepper to taste
1 tablespoon unsalted butter, softened
1 1/2 teaspoons sour cream

SUCCOTASH

1 small sweet onion, finely diced
4 cloves of garlic, minced
2 tablespoons butter
1 cup yellow corn kernels (about 2 ears)
1/2 cup fresh black-eyed peas
1/2 cup baby lima beans or butter beans
1/4 cup fresh okra, cut into ¼-inch slices
1/2 cup vegetable stock
Kosher salt and black pepper to taste

BLISTERED TOMATOES

2 pints cherry tomatoes
2 tablespoons extra virgin olive oil
1/2 cup balsamic vinegar
Kosher salt and black pepper to taste

GULF BLACK GROUPER

2 ounces light olive oil
4 (6-ounce) gulf black grouper fillets
Kosher salt and black pepper
4 sprigs of fresh thyme
2 tablespoons unsalted butter

FOR THE CORN PUDDING: Combine the stock and corn in a high speed blender container. Process until puréed; strain through a fine strainer. Pour into a double boiler. Season with salt and pepper. Cook over medium heat until thickened and of a thin pudding consistency, stirring frequently. Remove from the heat and stir in the butter and sour cream.

FOR THE SUCCOTASH: Sauté the onion and garlic in the butter in a heavy bottomed saucepan over medium-high heat until the onion is translucent, stirring constantly. Reduce the heat to medium. Add the corn. Cook for 3 to 4 minutes, stirring occasionally. Add the peas, beans, okra and stock. Season with salt and pepper. Cook until stock has almost evaporated.

FOR THE BLISTERED TOMATOES: Wash the tomatoes thoroughly and combine with the remaining ingredients in a large shallow baking dish. Broil under high heat for 2 to 3 minutes or until the tomato skins begin to crack. Let stand, covered with foil, for 20 minutes. May reheat by baking, covered, in a warm oven for 20 minutes or by gently reheating in a sauté pan.

FOR THE GULF BLACK GROUPER: Heat a large nonstick skillet over medium-high heat. Add the oil. Season the grouper with salt and pepper and add to the skillet gently. Cook for 3 minutes; turn. Add the thyme and butter to the pan. Cook for 3 minutes longer or just until the fish tests done.

TO SERVE: Layer the corn pudding, succotash, 3 or 4 of the blistered tomatoes and 1 grouper fillet in each of 4 warmed shallow bowls.

Serves 4

Grayton Beach

Grayton Beach has lured visitors with its beauty and tranquility since the days of travel by horse and buggy. Grayton Beach came to be thanks to Army Major Charles Gray, who built a home in the area around 1885. In 1890, Point Washington residents CSA Brigade General William Miller and William Wilson platted Grayton, naming it in honor of Gray. In the 1920s the Butler family purchased Grayton Beach with the intent of creating a vacation resort. Meanwhile, just up the road at Western Lake, the Miller family were grazing thousands of cattle and hogs. (If you look closely while walking on the bike path in Grayton Beach, you will see a sign identifying the old Miller homestead on Western Lake.) Thankfully, the herds of cattle were moved north to Freeport, and the Butler family began selling lots and homes. Nowadays Grayton is the type of place where neighbors still hand out free "Grayton Beach: Nice Dogs, Strange People" bumper stickers, locals stop by the coffee shop for hugs, and folks wait patiently for hours outside of The Red Bar to get a taste of 30A's most famous crab cakes.

Helping to keep Grayton wild is the 2,000-acre state park which almost surrounds it. Grayton Beach State Park and the Point Washington State Forest border Grayton, which means you might just spot a roving bear, deer or wild boar as the sun begins to set. Locals have dubbed one curious black bear "the Grayton bear" because he has been so often in the area.

Grayton Beach State Park is one of Florida's most awarded parks. The largest of 30A's coastal dune lakes, Western Lake, is partially located within the state park land. It normally forms a shallow pool near the crashing waves of the Gulf, creating a kid-friendly place to play and snorkel while mom and dad soak up the sun.

Because large parts of the beach are preserved as state park, you will find towering sand dunes bordering the waters of Western Lake and the Gulf of Mexico. And because Grayton Beach is one of two beaches in South Walton where driving on the beach is allowed by permit, it is common to tailgate with groups of friends in between casting a fishing line into the Gulf or cooling off in the shallow waters of the lake.

Once you are in town, slow down, explore the streets of Grayton by bicycle and indulge in a sunset that you will not soon forget. Grayton Beach is special and just a tad weird — and that is exactly how the locals like it.

30A *Tip*
TAKE A WALK ON THE STATE PARK'S MOST SOUTHERN TRAIL. HERE YOU WILL FIND A PRAYER OF THE WOODS AND A COOL PLACE TO REST HIDDEN UNDERNEATH THE SCRUB OAK IN A THRIVING DUNE SYSTEM.

DEAD FISH

Crab Bisque

Hurricane Oyster Bar & Grill

GRAYTON BEACH

1	pound (2 cups) butter		3	quarts (12 cups) heavy cream
2	stalks celery, finely diced		2	tablespoons chopped fresh basil
1	carrot, peeled, minced		1 1/2	teaspoons white pepper
6	shallots, minced		1 1/2	teaspoons cayenne pepper
4	cups flour		2	pounds crab claw meat, lobster, shrimp, or a combination
2	cups sherry			Salt to taste
1	pound lobster base			Chopped green onions for garnishing
4	quarts (1 gallon) water			
3	quarts (12 cups) half and half			

Melt the butter in a large stockpot over low heat. Add the celery, carrot and shallots. Sauté until softened. Whisk in the flour to make a roux. Cook over low heat until the flour has a nutty aroma, whisking constantly. Whisk in the sherry. Whisk in the lobster base until incorporated. Adjust the heat to medium low. Add the water, half and half, and heavy cream; mix well. Bring to a boil and cook until thickened, whisking constantly to prevent scorching. Fold in the seasonings and crab meat. Add a small amount of water if mixture is too thick. Season with salt to taste. Garnish with chopped green onions.

Serves 12 or more

Honey Roasted Granola

Another Broken Egg

GRAYTON BEACH AND SANDESTIN

2	cups quick-cooking (1-minute) plain dry oats	1/4	cup 80/20 olive oil
3/4	cup chopped pecans or pecan pieces	1/4	cup honey
1/3	cup sliced or chopped almonds	2	tablespoons apple juice
1	tablespoon loosely packed brown sugar	1/2	teaspoon vanilla extract
1/4	teaspoon each ground cinnamon and salt	1	cup raisins (optional)

Combine the oats, pecans, almonds, brown sugar, cinnamon, and salt in a large mixing bowl. (Do not add raisins.) Mix the olive oil, honey, apple juice, and vanilla in a small bowl. Add to the oatmeal mixture and mix well with a rubber spatula. Spread evenly on a parchment-lined full sheet baking pan.

Bake in a preheated 325-degree oven for 15 to 30 minutes, checking and stirring every 10 to 15 minutes until the mixture just begins to brown. Let cool on a wire rack. Add the raisins and stir to distribute evenly.

Makes 4 cups with raisins

Scooter's Mini Crab Cakes with Remoulade

Grayton Beach Catering

GRAYTON BEACH

MINI CRAB CAKES

8	to 16 ounces fresh lump crab meat
1/3	cup light mayonnaise
3	green onions, thinly sliced
1	teaspoon Stinky's seafood seasoning
1	teaspoon Worcestershire sauce
2	large eggs
3	slices Sarah Lee whole grain bread
	Remoulade Sauce

Combine crab meat, mayonnaise, green onions, seasonings, and eggs in a bowl; mix lightly. Process the bread in a food processor. Add to the crab mixture; mix lightly. Shape into half dollar-sized patties. Fry in olive oil in a skillet until golden brown, turning once. Serve with a dollop of Remoulade Sauce and garnish with chopped green onion.

REMOULADE SAUCE

2	cups mayonnaise
1/4	cup Creole mustard
2	large cloves of garlic, pressed
2	tablespoons chopped fresh parsley
1	tablespoon lemon juice
2 1/4	teaspoons smoked paprika
3/4	teaspoon ground red pepper

Combine all ingredients in a bowl. Whisk to combine. Store in the refrigerator, covered, for 2 hours to 3 days.

30A's Coastal Dune Lakes

WESTERN LAKE

CAMP CREEK LAKE

Deer Lake

Blue Mountain Beach

Blue Mountain Beach is the highest elevation found along Florida's Gulf Coast, which means it also has the best views. So why the unusual name? Well, early sailors christened it Blue Mountain after seeing its high sand dunes covered in the rare blooms of the Blue Lupine flower (which are blue and still flower in the area).

A small community with a neighborly feel, Blue Mountain Beach has a popular ice cream shop, a natural foods store, bike rentals, a bakery and delicious restaurants. The community is also home to two rare coastal dune lakes and connects to nature trails in the Point Washington State Forest and the bike path along Scenic 30A. The vibe in Blue Mountain Beach is laid-back, relaxed and friendly. Families often walk up from the beach to grab an ice cream cone or fresh fruit smoothie and the restaurants here serve some of the finest fried shrimp on 30A.

The meandering warm waters of Big Red Fish Lake are perfect for introducing little ones to the water when the waves in the Gulf are too rough. Narrow neighborhood streets and friendly locals evoke the feel of Old Florida and help you remember what a beach vacation is all about.

Mile-High Four Fish Salad

Local Catch Bar & Grill — CHEF ADAM YELLIN

BLUE MOUNTAIN BEACH

FOR EACH SERVING

Spring lettuce mix

Fresh pico de gallo or a mixture of chopped fresh
tomatoes, onion and jalapeno peppers marinated
in cane vinegar and salt and pepper

Pineapple salsa or a mixture of chopped fresh
pineapple, red bell pepper, and red onion
marinated in cane vinegar and salt and pepper

Balsamic vinaigrette to taste(optional)

Grilled fish of choice

Creole seasoning to taste

Toast points

Mound the spring lettuce mix on a serving plate. Top with pico de gallo or the marinated tomato mixture. Spoon the pineapple salsa or the marinated fresh pineapple mixture on top. Drizzle with the balsamic vinaigrette if desired. Serve with grilled fish, a sprinkle of Creole seasoning and toast points.

Note: If you include the juices from the fresh pico de gallo and salsa, no other dressing may be necessary.

Seared Tuna Salad with Ginger Dressing

Marie's Bistro
BLUE MOUNTAIN BEACH

FOR YOUR OWN GINGER DRESSING

1/4	cup rice vinegar	2	tablespoons grated fresh ginger
1/4	cup olive oil	1	teaspoon salt
1	tablespoon honey		

Combine all ingredients in a medium bowl; mix well. Chill in the refrigerator for 30 minutes or longer.

FOR THE TUNA SALAD

1	12-ounce Ahi tuna steak	1	medium cucumber, sliced
Salt and pepper to taste		2	medium Roma tomatoes, sliced
8	ounces artisan lettuce, chopped	1	small carrot, shredded
8	ounces romaine lettuce, chopped	1	avocado, sliced

Heat a sauté pan over high heat until very hot. Season the tuna on both sides with salt and pepper. Sauté for 1 minute on each side for rare or 2 minutes on each side for medium-rare. Remove the tuna and set aside to rest. Combine the lettuce, romaine, cucumber, tomatoes, and carrot in a large salad bowl. Top with the avocado slices. Drizzle with the ginger dressing.

Serves 4

GULF PLACE

*G*ulf Place is a one-stop shop for all your beach fun. Here you will find quirky beach art, fresh local fish, fashion perfect for the beach, and wonderful condominiums with views of the Gulf. Across the street is Ed Walline Park, one of 30A's largest public beach accesses. Surrounding Gulf Place are beach homes and nearby is Santa Rosa Golf & Beach Club. It's a great spot to enjoy lunch while breathing in the fresh, salt air. On the weekends Gulf Place hosts art shows, and seasonal events on the large lawn. Stop by for lunch or spend the week: there is always something to do at Gulf Place.

DUNE ALLEN BEACH

*D*une Allen Beach looks a bit like time has stood still. Granted, new homes have sprung up around Oyster Lake and the beachfront is a bit more crowded than it used to be, but here in Dune Allen you can still get a sense for what the beach must have been like before 30A was discovered.

Small cinderblock beach cottages and a laid-back attitude help this little beach town stay true to its roots. Located at the western entrance to Scenic 30A, Dune Allen gives you that fresh taste of Florida and sets the stage for the beauty of the drive ahead of you. Dunes and views of a coastal dune lake intersperse with classic beach cottages and larger rental homes.

Spend the day at the beach and then head over to one of the great neighborhood restaurants for fresh caught Gulf fish and a great time.

Warm Bacon Dressing

Stinky's Fish Camp — CHEF BRANNON JANCA
DUNE ALLEN BEACH

(STINKY'S SIZE)

2	cups fat-rendered minced bacon
1/4	cup caraway seed
2	cups minced onion
1	cup sugar
3	cups rice wine vinegar
1	tablespoon poppy seed
2	quarts chicken stock
1	quart peanut oil
3	cups Dijon mustard
1/2	cup cornstarch
2	cups chicken stock

(FAMILY SIZE)

1/4	cup fat-rendered minced bacon
1 1/2	teaspoons caraway seed
1/4	cup minced onion
2	tablespoons sugar
6	tablespoons rice wine vinegar
3/8	teaspoon poppy seed
1	cup chicken stock
1/4	cup peanut oil
6	tablespoons Dijon mustard
1	tablespoons cornstarch
1/4	cup chicken stock

Sauté the bacon in a saucepan until crisp. Add the caraway seed and sauté until toasty brown. Add the onion and sauté until translucent. Add the sugar, vinegar, poppy seed, 2 quarts (1 cup) stock and oil. Simmer for 20 minutes. Blend the mustard, cornstarch and remaining chicken stock in a small bowl. Stir into the bacon mixture. Simmer for 10 minutes, stirring constantly.

Yield: 1 gallon at Stinky's: about 2 cups at home

Scallops in Mango Butter Sauce

Vue on 30a
DUNE ALLEN BEACH

FOR EACH SERVING

4	ounces white wine
3	ounces white vinegar
4	ounces heavy cream

1	mango, peeled, cut into chunks
6	ounces (6 tablespoons) butter
2	pieces bacon
4	scallops

Combine the wine, vinegar, cream and mango in a saucepan. Simmer until the mixture is reduced by ½. Pour into a blender container and process until smooth. Return the mixture to the saucepan. Whisk in the butter over medium heat; set aside and keep warm. Preheat the oven to 375 degrees.

Place the bacon on a baking sheet. Bake for 14 minutes or until crisp. Pan sear the scallops in a small amount of oil in a hot sauté pan for 1 minute on each side or until golden brown. Place on a serving pate. Spoon the mango sauce over the scallops. Top with crumbled bacon.

GRAND BOULEVARD

Scenic 30A was only missing one thing—an amazing movie theater. While it is not on 30A, Grand Boulevard is just a short drive to the west. Here you will find Boulevard 10, which features the Big D 3D experience screen and the Ovation Dining Club, which lets you enjoy the latest movie while dining on fresh Gulf shrimp and enjoying a nice glass of wine. Home to South Walton's Fashion Week, Grand Boulevard combines spacious lush lawns, towering palms and an arcade of shops to create a shopping experience to remember. A large splash fountain gives the kids a place to cool off and burn off energy. An Aveda salon, a children's boutique and small art galleries round out the shopping experience at this beautiful outdoor mall.

SANDESTIN

Sandestin is a massive resort within a resort located just a few miles from Scenic 30A. Here you will find golf courses, beachfront hotels, one of the area's only full-service spas, restaurants and a mix of hotels, condominiums and single family homes. The 2,400- acre property fronts the beach and backs into Choctawhatchee Bay. It's a location that allows for quick access from Sandestin's docks to the deep waters of the Pass in Destin.

Championship golf courses and the mini-entertainment district in the Village of Baytowne Wharf are open to the public. The remainder of the property is private and available only to Sandestin homeowners and guests.

Baytowne offers a fantastic place for families to go and play. A zip line, climbing walls, an arcade and numerous restaurants create a miniature town that provides all the fun you can handle in one day. At night the town transforms into a place to dance and have fun. A boardwalk leads away from Baytowne Wharf through the trees bordering the Bay. If you look closely you'll find a pirate fort hidden amongst the oaks.

30A *Tip*
HEAD OVER TO
JOLEE ISLAND
FOR BREATHTAKING
VIEWS.

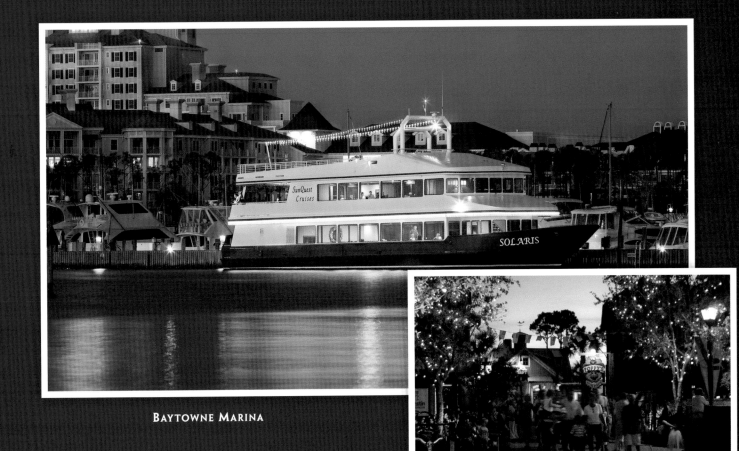

Baytowne Marina

The Village of Baytowne Wharf

Blue Crab and Lemon Ravioli with Shellfish Sauce

Seagar's Prime Steaks and Seafood — CHEF DAN VARGO

SANDESTIN

THIS RECIPE WAS THE PEOPLE'S CHOICE WINNER IN THE 2013 "30A THROWDOWN"

FOR THE SHELLFISH SAUCE

2	ounces blended oil		2	tablespoons tomato paste
1	cup shrimp shells		1/4	cup white wine
1/4	yellow onion, chopped		4	cups water
2	tablespoons each chopped celery, carrot, tomato, and tomato paste		1	tablespoon whole tarragon
			1	lemon, peel and pith removed
1/2	teaspoon black peppercorns		1	bay leaf

Heat the oil in a saucepan. Add the shrimp shells. Sauté until shells turn pink. Add the celery, carrot, tomato and peppercorns. Cook for 5 minutes. Stir in the tomato paste. Cook for 3 to 4 minutes; do not stir. Add the wine, stirring to deglaze the pan. Add the water. Simmer for 25 minutes; remove from the heat. Add the tarragon, lemon and bay leaf. Let stand for 20 minutes to infuse. Strain through a fine mesh sieve; keep warm.

FOR THE LEMON PASTA

8	ounces cake flour		Zest of 1/4 lemon
1	egg yolk		Kosher salt to taste
1/2	ounce virgin olive oil		

Shape the flour into a mound. Make a well in the center. Mix the egg yolk with the remaining ingredients and pour into the flour well. Working from the center out, combine to form a dough and knead for 5 to 8 minutes or until smooth, adding additional flour to the surface as needed. Let dough rest, covered with a towel, for 25 minutes. Roll out with pasta roller to last setting just before filling. Cut into 2 large squares.

FOR THE CRAB MEAT FILLING

1/2 tablespoon minced shallot	1/4 teaspoon minced parsley
2 tablespoons (1 ounce) butter	2 ounces Mascarpone cheese
4 ounces Blue Crab meat, picked over	1 1/2 ounces Asiago cheese, shredded
Zest and juice of 1/4 lemon	Salt and pepper to taste
1/2 teaspoon each minced tarragon and parsley	Egg wash for sealing

Sauté the shallot in the butter in a saucepan until softened; remove from the heat. Fold in the remaining ingredients; mix well. Spoon onto one ravioli square; brush edges with egg wash. Top with the remaining pasta, pressing to seal edges; trim with pasta cutter. Cook in boiling salted water in a saucepan for 2 to 3 minutes; drain.

FOR THE PLATING SAUCE

2 tablespoons butter	Zest of 1/4 lemon
1/2 tablespoon minced shallot	1 tablespoon mixed tarragon and parsley
1 1 1/2-ounce tomato, seeded, cut into small dice	1/4 ounce baby arugula

Melt 1 tablespoon butter in a saucepan. Add the shallot. Cook until translucent. Add the tomato and 1 portion of the shellfish sauce. Bring to a simmer. Add the ravioli. Swirl in the lemon zest, herbs and remaining butter. Season with salt and pepper to taste. Place the ravioli in a serving bowl. Spoon the sauce over the ravioli and garnish with the baby arugula.

MIRAMAR BEACH

Are you looking for a beach drive that showcases some of the most beautiful beaches in Walton County? Head down Scenic Gulf View Drive in Miramar Beach and take in the views from the wide public beach accesses. Here you'll find parasailing, jet ski rentals and a taste of Florida that you might have forgotten still existed. Locals and tourists enjoy a lifestyle which includes restaurants and world-class shopping (one of the largest designer outlet malls in the nation is in Miramar Beach) within steps of the sugar-white sand. Miramar Beach is also a popular surfing spot for locals. The next time a storm approaches the area, grab a camera (or a surf board) and head on down to the beach. Even if you don't get in the water, you'll have plenty of entertainment for the day.

30A Fruit Soup

Signature Catering of 30A — CHEF CHRISTOPHER LEVI HOLBROOK
SANTA ROSA BEACH

To prepare the Fruit Soup, the recipe must be completed in two parts: first prepare the fruits for the soup. Second, create the sorbet and Champagne "soup." Combine right before serving.

FOR THE FRUIT

Peaches

Plutos

Kiwi

Papaya

Honeycomb Mango

Whole Raspberries and Blueberries

Scoop out the peaches, plutos, kiwi, papaya, and mango with a melon ball scoop. Combine with the berries in a serving bowl. Chill, covered, until serving time.

FOR THE SOUP

2   pints lemon sorbet

1   bottle of chilled Champagne

2   tablespoons vanilla bean paste

Valencia orange sorbet, vanilla bean oil and fresh mint for garnishing

Just before serving, combine the lemon sorbet, Champagne and vanilla bean paste in a bowl; mix well. Pour over the fruit. Garnish with Valencia orange sorbet, vanilla bean oil, and fresh mint. (**For the Vanilla Bean oil**, blend 3 tablespoons vanilla bean paste and 4 ounces canola oil.)

Red Beans and Rice

The Marigny
SANTA ROSA BEACH

2 cups finely diced yellow onion	1 teaspoon salt
2 cups finely diced celery	1 teaspoon white pepper
1 cup finely diced bell pepper	1 tablespoon black pepper
2 cups sliced green onions	1/2 teaspoon cayenne pepper
1/2 cup minced garlic	1 smoked ham hock
4 cups chopped ham	2 pounds Camelia brand red beans
1 cup bacon drippings	Chicken or beef stock
1 pound andouille sausage, cut into 1/4-inch slices	1 cup chopped parsley
1 teaspoon each dried thyme and dried whole oregano	2 cups sliced green onions
	2 cups Louisiana popcorn rice

Sauté the first 4 vegetables, garlic and ham in the bacon drippings in a large stockpot until tender. Add the sausage, herbs, seasonings, and ham hock. Add the beans; stir to mix well. Add enough stock to cover the mixture by 2 inches. Bring to a rolling boil. Cook for 30 minutes, stirring occasionally. Reduce the heat to low. Simmer for 2 hours longer. Remove from the heat. Add the parsley and the remaining 2 cups sliced green onions. Adjust the seasonings; keep warm. Bring 4 cups water to a boil in a saucepan. Add the rice. Bring to a boil. Bake, covered with a tight lid, at 350 degrees for 20 minutes. Serve the red beans over the rice.

Serves 8

Sesame-Crusted Rare Tuna

Cafe Thirty-A — CHEF KEN DUENAS

1¹/2 tablespoons sesame oil plus more for sautéing
6¹/2 tablespoons soy sauce
1/2 cup black sesame seeds
1/2 cup white sesame seeds
1 12-ounce fresh #1 yellowfin or bluefin tuna loin
Salt and pepper to taste
1 teaspoon grated fresh gingerroot
1 teaspoon chopped garlic

1 tablespoon chopped green onion
1/2 cup roughly chopped Napa cabbage
1/2 cup each julienne red bell pepper, red onion, and red cabbage
1/4 cup julienne carrots
Pickled ginger and wasabi paste for garnishing (available at grocery stores or Asian specialty markets)

Combine the 1¹/2 tablespoons sesame oil and the soy sauce in a small bowl, whisking to combine. Toss 2 tablespoons of the blend with the sesame seeds in a small bowl; set aside. Cut the tuna into 2 portions. Season with salt and pepper. Coat each with the sesame seed mixture; set aside. Sauté the gingerroot, garlic and green onion in a small amount of smoking-hot sesame oil in a wok or skillet for 10 seconds. Add the remaining vegetables. Cook for 2 minutes longer or until tender-crisp. Season with salt and pepper and a splash of the remaining sesame oil blend. Remove from the heat. Heat several tablespoons of sesame oil in a sauté pan until smoking hot. Place the tuna carefully in the pan. Sear for 30 seconds on each side or until nicely colored but rare inside. Slice into thin pieces. Spoon the vegetables onto serving plates. Arrange the tuna on top. Garnish with pickled ginger and wasabi paste.

If less rare tuna is desired, place the skillet in a 350-degree oven and bake until done to taste.

Serves 2

CHOCTAWHATCHEE BAY

30A SONGWRITERS FESTIVAL   JANUARY

Begin the year right by attending the annual 30A Songwriters Festival. The festival lineup changes each year, but past festivals have included chart topping artists like Matthew Sweet, Shawn Mullins, Emily Saliers, John Oates and Joe Leathers. Of course, being 30A, this Songwriters Festival is a little different from most festivals around the country. The venues are small, the artists are open and generous about sharing the stories behind the making of their songs, and the air almost crackles with inspiration and energy as the performances get underway. One of the best aspects of the festival is how artists, both chart-topping and fledgling, relax and just seem to have fun rocking the crowds. Different artists will often decide on a whim to perform together and that is when the magic happens. As you relax on a towel spread across the lawn at Alys Beach or look out at the view of the Gulf from Fish Out of Water in WaterColor, you get to see the seeds of new songs being planted and ideas for future albums being formed. It's an experience that you can't find anywhere else.

www.30asongwritersfestival.com

ESCAPE TO CREATE JANUARY/FEBRUARY

The Escape to Create artist-in-residency program in Seaside gives artists a chance to step away from the tedium of their normal day-to-day schedules and spend a few weeks, sometimes months, focusing on only their art. The residency provides housing and a small stipend and in return locals and visitors to 30A are treated to free concerts, plays, readings, songwriting sessions and much more. Past residency attendees have included author Scott Morris and playwright Rich Orloff, who have gone on to publish and produce the book and plays finished while enjoying time along 30A.

www.escape2create.org

SEASIDE SCHOOL HALF MARATHON & 5K RUN   MARCH

Get ready to run for a great cause! The Seaside School Half Marathon & 5K Run benefits the Seaside Neighborhood School (Florida's first charter school). Students at this award-winning middle school participate in an annual robotics competition (for which it has won state honors), grow and tend their own organic garden and even host a community radio show. The race itself offers a 5K and Half Marathon course for runners. The 5K course extends from Seaside to the Grayton State Park entrance and back, while Half Marathon runners continue all the way down 30A to Gulf Place before returning to Seaside. Post race celebrations include medals for the Half Marathon runners, awards for fastest times, free barbecue and beer and bags from the races major sponsor, Vera Bradley. Race entries are limited, so sign up quickly to ensure a number.

www.snsrun.com

ARTSQUEST MAY

The ArtsQuest Fine Arts Festival is a juried festival with a long history along 30A. Past festivals have been held at Eden Gardens State Park, Sandestin, Seaside, Grayton Beach and WaterColor. You'll find fine oil paintings, stunning photography, handmade jewelry, pottery, carvings and more. It's a great place to shop for those special gifts that can never be duplicated or found anywhere else. The festival also gives you a chance to meet and spend time talking to the artists about their process, inspiration and craft.

www.artsquestflorida.com

DIGITAL GRAFFITI

Do you need to funk it up a bit? If you are looking for an event that is inspiring, fun, different and well … funky … then go ahead and mark Digital Graffiti down in your calendar. Digital Graffiti combines art, music, mood and lighting in a way that can't be found anywhere else in the world. The art moves, shifts and changes while being projected onto the white stucco walls of homes in Alys Beach. The juried festival awards cash prizes for winning entries and culminates with one of the best dance parties on 30A. Revelers enjoy a DJ and interactive art projections while taking in the beauty of Alys Beach's Caliza Pool. It's one of the best parties of the year.

www.digitalgraffiti.com

30A FOURTH OF JULY PARADE

The Fourth of July Parade is one of 30A's most treasured events. This small town parade features decorated golf carts, dogs in costume, choreographed dance routines and locals and the vacationers who love 30A. It is everyone's parade. You'll see floats from your favorite shop, catch candy tossed from a family who has been vacationing here for five generations and delight at the fun involved with something as simple as a hometown parade. The kids love it and the grown-ups love it even more. The parade helps ground 30A and reminds us all how simple life really is. The route begins in Seagrove and continues west to Seaside. Anyone may participate by filling out an application in advance.

SANDESTIN TRIATHLON   AUGUST

"Each year athletes converge on Sandestin to challenge to challenge their bodies and their minds with a half-mile swim in the Gulf of Mexico, a four-mile run along the beach and Choctawhatchee Bay and a 20-mile bike ride. The biking portion of the race includes 30A (from Dune Allen to Blue Mountain Beach). So, if you aren't quite up to participating in the triathlon, you can cheer on these warrior men and women and give them a proper 30A welcome.

www.sandestintriathlon.com

SOUTH WALTON FASHION WEEK OCTOBER

Each October South Walton's finest designers and local boutiques show the latest looks during a large-scale, high-fashion event that has become one of the most eagerly anticipated weeks of the year.

South Walton Fashion Week is presented by Visit South Walton and produced by the Cultural Arts Alliance of Walton County, in partnership with Monark Events and Grand Boulevard. Net proceeds benefit the Arts in Education program of the Cultural Arts Alliance of Walton County.

SEEING RED WINE FESTIVAL   NOVEMBER

Do you love wine? Have you ever been to a wine festival that offered more than 800 wines? Get ready to pace yourself and enjoy the Seeing Red Wine Festival's full schedule of tastings, vintner dinners, chef demonstrations and more. The Festival offers events held at several different locations throughout South Walton, including Sandestin and Grand Boulevard, but culminates with the outdoor Seeing Red Wine Festival in Seaside. Here you will have a chance to meet vintners, enjoy the weather, relax and spend the day in Seaside sampling wines in the amphitheater and Ruskin Place.

www.seeingredwinefestival.com

SOUTH WALTON FASHION WEEK

30A HOLIDAY PARADE NOVEMBER

Locals loved the 30A Fourth of July parade so much they decided to create a Christmas parade too. The parade has the same small-town fun as the Fourth of July parade, but this time you get to see Santa and Mrs. Claus, sip on hot chocolate and ooh and ahh as the Christmas lights are turned on in Seaside. Be sure to bring your camera to this one.

CHRISTMAS AT EDEN DECEMBER

Eden Gardens State Park is one of Florida's most awarded state parks. Each Christmas the Friends of Eden organization hosts a candlelight event and tour of the Eden Mansion to raise funds for the popular park. Seeing the Mansion bedecked in wreaths, bows and Christmas trees is a great way to get in the holiday spirit. Many locals use the Christmas at Eden tour as their official kick-off to Christmas event. Families are welcome and kids love it. A nominal entry fee is required.

NEW YEAR'S EVE

Is there anything better than fireworks exploding over the Gulf? 30A shimmers and booms each New Year's Eve with huge firework shows taking place in Rosemary Beach, Alys Beach, Seaside and Sandestin. The beach is also lit up with the gold fizz of sparklers as families relax and enjoy watching all four firework shows at once. On a clear night you can even see the red, gold and blue fireworks exploding over Panama City Beach's Pier Park and the Harborwalk Village in Destin. Remember, it is illegal to shoot off your own fireworks in Florida. Only sparklers are allowed. So dig your toes in the sand and ooh and ahh at the professional shows going off all along the coast.

Credits

Susan Vallée is the owner of Bennett Vallée Communications, LLC and one of 30A's biggest fans. When not writing about life along Florida's most scenic highway, she is trying to enjoy it.

Photographer Brandan Babineaux has been capturing the beauty of 30A for years. While he loves architectural and landscape shots, he says he prefers to shoot candid, life-on-the-move photographs and can often be seen around 30A with a camera in hand. See his work at www.brandanbabineaux.com.

Inside *Meet me on 30A* are breath–taking images shot by South Walton's finest photographers. The Southwestern Publishing Group would like to acknowledge the beautiful contributions from these talented photographers. For a listing of each photographer, please see page 2.

Special Places

Recipe Index

Recipe Index

For more information

VISIT US AT
30A.COM